Pressing On
to
Maturity

The Church's Need
To Refocus On The
Eternal Pathway

Roger Alliman, M.A.

Scripture passages are taken from a variety of translations and
paraphrases to include The New King James Version,
the New American Standard Version, The New Living Translation,
the Amplified Bible, the J.B. Phillips New Testament,
and The Message. In many cases the author often used his own
paraphrase in an effort to enhance the meaning within his context.
Any underlining of portions of scripture are for emphasis only
by the author.

Contents

....let us press on to maturity, not laying again a foundation of repentance from dead works and of faith toward God...
(Hebrews 6:1)

Introduction & Acknowledgements

Let us leave the elementary teaching
about the Christ, and let us press on to maturity,
not laying again a foundation of repentance
from dead works and of faith toward God....
Hebrews 6:1

*Since you have been raised to new life with Christ,
set your sights on the realities of heaven, where Christ
sits in the place of honor at God's right hand.
Think about the things of heaven, not the things of
earth. For you have died and your real life is
hidden with Christ in God.
And when Christ, who is your life, is revealed
to the whole world, you will share in all his glory.*
Colossians 3:1-4

Over my forty-plus years as a Christian, I have seldom heard what you are about to read taught, or preached from the pulpit.

I have two seminary degrees, one in Biblical Studies and a graduate degree in Christian Counseling. In my studies for those two degrees, I never heard or read what you will be reading.

I have read hundreds of Christian books on how to live the Christian life and what God has done for us as believers. Only a few of those books touched the tip of what should be Basic 101 for all Christians in my view.

You're probably thinking, "What a pride filled, arrogant, holier-than-thou guy this is." I, of course, deny that and just ask you to open your heart to what the Scriptures tell us and what that should mean for us as a child of God. How should that impact our view of who we are? How should that effect our behavior? Should we adjust the way we see God, to include how he relates to us—in both positive and what appear to be negative ways?

I want to challenge some deeply held beliefs you might have. Like most Christians....

> # ....we can profess many things (head) but we tend to live what we believe (heart).

....if you confess with your mouth Jesus as Lord, <u>and believe in your heart</u> that God raised Him from the dead, you will be saved. (Romans 10:9)

God's word is the ultimate truth. I believe our challenge is to receive it, letting the indwelling Spirit of God shape our thinking, as we do everything we can to trust it, rely on it, and let it permeate our very soul as we learn to better understand why God has chosen to give his very LIFE to his children.

Over the course of my Christian life I have been largely impacted by the teaching of five men. These five men introduced me to what some Christians would call "the deeper life." That has a ring of eliteism if you will, so I would prefer to call it what Watchman Nee called it—*The Normal Christian Life,* the title of one of his many books. Nee was a Christian leader in the early 20th century, was persecuted and imprisoned for his faith, and spent the last twenty years of his life in prison.

The five men who I hold dear to my heart for their teaching, their personal friendship, and their example of that mature life were pastors and leaders Peter Lord, DeVern Fromke, and Jack Taylor, along with seminary professor and leader Dr. Victor Matthews, and my good friend Lee LeFebre whose counselor training organization board of directors I served on for over twenty-five years.

As I studied and taught the scriptures after my conversion over forty years ago, I couldn't get enough of the Bible and learning about God's ways and his unyielding truths on matters of life, righteousness, and living under his umbrella of love, mercy, patience, and grace.

Over the years we have attended many churches of several evangelical denominations, and I am always disappointed at how little of the more penetrating truths of God's word are actually taught to the body of Christ. Again I don't want to sound elitist, but as I search through commentaries and the writings of many leaders of our faith, our seminaries, and our churches— I don't find much teaching on what should be some of the most important basic information a believer can learn and understand about what God has done on our behalf as his children.

Nearly all seminaries seem to avoid the basic distinction between spirit, soul, and body. Distinctions that the Apostle Paul and the writer of Hebrews clearly pointed out as an underlying force in our personal understanding of what God has done on our behalf, and how he is always pressing us forward toward maturity on the path of righteousness. This is not something that we must wait for in the age to come, but much of that completeness is for his people right now, today, as we rest in his faithfulness and promises of the wholeness that he has given his children for this life. For now. The present. Today.

Finally, Part III includes a concept that was first exposed to me by Mr. Fromke, a dear and gracious gentleman who has been given remarkable insights into the marvelous fatherhood of our God. His concept of our movement from child to son was immensely meaningful to me nearly forty years ago. I have taken the liberty to relate the essence of his views along with my expanded version of a graphic that he used in his book *Ultimate Intention* which you can purchase at his website: http://fromke.com/.

I was first introduced to Mr. Fromke by my wonderful friend and mentor, Peter Lord. These pastoral friends have not only taught thousands the pure and faithful principles that God has made available to us, but more importantly they have given us living examples of what it means to be a follower of Jesus Christ. Examples of what I believe to be a focused pathway to a better understanding of God's ways with us and his desire that we press on to Christian Maturity.

I was blessed to have all of these men in my life during my years as a believer.

Thank you, Father.

— *Roger Alliman*

Part I

Identity & Behavior

God has given you the whole world to use,
and life and even death are your servants.
He has given you all of the present and all of
the future. All are yours, and you belong
to Christ, and Christ is God's.
1 Corinthians 3:22-23

If I said to you, "If you're a sinner, raise your hand," you would likely raise your hand. If I then said, "Tell me your last sin," chances are very good that you would have to think before you could answer. We have been led to believe that, "There just has to be many things I've done wrong in God's eyes today...."

And even when you come up with a particular action that you consider could be a sin, it is likely something marginal like, "I got angry with the cashier at the store because the price on the milk was not right when I checked out." Was that really a sin? Whether you think it was or not, do you still consider yourself a sinner?

The body of Christ in the modern church environment suffers from an unmistakable case of *Identity Theft*. There is a pervading "such a worm as I" mentality in much of the modern church. We, of course, fall short of the glory and perfection of God, but is it really "such a worm as I?"

We in the United States, of course, live in a culture that chooses to see identity as what you do, where you live, who you know, what you drive—all based on performance and behavior.

If you achieved good grades in school, went to college, married someone with a good background, live in a nice neighborhood, and have stellar goals for your life and your children—then you must be a really good person.

If your grades in school were marginal, you skipped college, you have gotten in trouble more than once with parents and authorities, you married someone with a similar background, and although you both have a pretty good job, times are hard and you seem to be living month to month financially, and you're still not sure if you really have a goal for your life. Well, sorry.... you seem to fall short of what both God and the world really expect of you, if you are to be counted among the accomplished and successful by the world's standards.

What Determines Value?

The world has it's own way of determining a person's identity and gauging a person's value? Certainly the Bible takes a different approach to establish worth, self-esteem, and potential for God's people.

As a Christian should I base my view of your worth and value on who you are as a person or should I base it on what I perceive to be your accomplishments and your behavior?

One is about who you are, the other is all about how you perform and what you achieve in accordance with certain pre-set standards that the world considers worthy of honor.

If you are known as a "good" Christian, should I base my view of your value and worth on the supposition that you're apparently a little better sinner than many other people I know?

Or should I base my view of your value on how God refers to you—as a Saint. Let me add, of course, a saint who occasionally sins.

The world says your performance and behavior determine your identity. But God says that if you're his child, then your very identity, who you are in Christ, determines your value, and ultimately your behavior.

Now—let me be clear..... we all sin on occasion. But that must not be seen as our identity. Is that sin a reflection of who we are, or a reflection of how we occasionally act?

Charles Trumbull said in his classic book, *Victory in Christ....*

> ## "It is not that the Christian is <u>not able</u> to sin, but it is that we are <u>able not</u> to sin."

We must remember, a believer is no longer a slave to sin. And what does the Bible say about all of this? Are we referred to as sinners? Or are we saints who sometimes sin?

Think about Paul's letters to the churches. Does he begin his letters with; "To all of you low down sinners at Ephesus" or to the Philippians, "To all you depraved worms at Philippi." No, of course not. He always referred to "...the saints at Ephesus," "the saints at Philippi," or "...to the Colossian saints."

What is at stake here is the totality and completeness of what God has done on our behalf.

When we believed, no matter our age, God changed our complete identity. We became someone we had never been before. Then to make it complete, God gave us his very life, in the person of the indwelling Holy Spirit.

To help complete our understanding of the totality of the change he made in us, he gave us the Bible. And in his book, he assures us that we are a saint, a new creation, elect, pure, holy, complete, righteous, and without blemish. This is not a hope, or a possibility, or even for a future time. This is a fact right now, the truth, an absolute from your heavenly father.

If self-esteem has been an issue in your life—whether positive or negative self-esteem, you must accept the reality that self-esteem is only an opinion—nothing more, and nothing less. And too many opinions are, more often than not, measured by the world's dysfunctional self-centered standards.

....if anyone is in Christ, that person is a new creation. The old things have gone away, and look, new things have arrived.... God caused the one who didn't know sin to be sin for our sake so that through him we could become the righteousness of God. (2 Corinthians 5:17, 21)

....he chose us to be, in Christ, his holy and blameless children living within his constant care. He planned, in his purpose of love, that we should be adopted as his own children through Jesus Christ—that we might learn to praise that glorious generosity of his which has made us welcome in the everlasting love he bears towards the Son. (Ephesians 1:4,6 Phillips)

Does Finished Really Mean Finished?

Here is something to think about. What does it mean when scripture tells us that we are complete.... holy.... righteous.... perfect? You might be thinking: "Well I still have lustful thoughts," or "I still get angry at our leaders in Washington," or " I still act selfishly & want my way much of the time." Oh my goodness—welcome to life on planet earth—welcome to the church.

In other words, you're saying you often struggle like Paul did in Romans 7 when he fussed that he does things he shouldn't and doesn't do things he should. In other words he was a saint that sometime sinned.

The desire to do good is inside of me, but I can't do it. I don't do the good that I want to do, but I do the evil that I don't want to do. I'm not the one doing it anymore, it is sin that lives in me.... (Romans 7:18-23)

Paul was telling us that....

...sin is a law, it operates 24/7 and we can't get away from it until we leave this planet.

Paul followed that statement with the reality....

I'm a miserable human being. Who will deliver me from this dead corpse? Thank God through Jesus Christ our Lord! So then, on the one hand I myself with my mind am serving the law of God, but on the other, with my flesh the law of sin. (Romans 7:24-26)

However, in dependence on the Holy Spirit within, and motivated by the reality of who I am—a child of the Creator God—I can rise above the law of sin and choose to do what I should, and choose to not do what I shouldn't. It is my choice. And, like Paul, I want my behavior to reflect my identity as a saint who belongs to the kingdom of God.

So to begin the process of that kind of change in our thinking, we have to be willing to separate our identity from our occasional bad behavior.

The world wants us on a track of doing in order to be. God has changed the whole process. His plan is, "I have changed who you are in order to change what you do."

Are We Really Spirit, Soul and Body?

Gradually over the years, our seminaries, our preachers and teachers, have forgotten that we were created as three-part beings. God was very clear in telling us that we are, by identity, <u>spirit</u>-beings, that express ourselves through our <u>soul</u> (mind-emotions-will), and are housed in a <u>body</u>.

God is three persons. We also are three-part beings. Paul made it a point in his letter to the Thessalonians:

....may your spirit, soul, and body be preserved blameless unto the coming of our Lord Jesus Christ. (1 Thessalonians 5:23)

The writer of Hebrews also made it a point to expose the difference between soul and spirit:

...the word of God is quick, and powerful, and sharper than any two-edged sword, piercing even to the dividing asunder of soul and spirit... (Hebrews 4:12)

Spirit – (Center)—The spiritual dimension—That is who we are, created in the image of God, spiritual beings.

Soul – (Head)—Our psychological dimension—Mind/Emotions/Will. How we think, feel, and make choices.

Body – (Body)—Our physical dimension—An earthly container, necessary for life on this planet.

Now.... If my primary identity is spiritual, then the entire purpose of God's original plan for us was not just the forgiveness of our sins, which was necessary to bring us back into a relationship with him. But it concluded that reconciliation with the mystery that Paul referred to—God's ultimate process in giving us his very LIFE, through the indwelling Holy Spirit who is now one with our spirit.

This mystery was first given to the prophet Ezekiel in chapter 36 where God explained the process that would accomplish the mystery of the New Covenant.

In my paraphrased wording, God's plan was.... *"I will take out your cold & stony heart and I will give you a new heart of flesh. Then I will give you a new spirit* (lower case s)*, and I will then put my Spirit* (upper case S) *within you."*

The New Testament writers made this a consistent point of reference for all believers. We must learn to understand the differences between spirit and soul and how one relates to who we are, the other relates to how we think, feel, and make decisions.

One With God's Spirit

<u>We have received God's Spirit</u> (not the world's spirit), so we can know the wonderful things God has freely given us. (1 Corinthians 2:12)

That He would grant you, according to the riches of His glory, to be strengthened with might through <u>His Spirit in the inner </u>man. (Ephesians 3:16)

> ## ...*the person who is joined to the Lord <u>is one spirit with him</u>.* (1 Corinthians 6:17)

His divine power has given to us all things that pertain to life and godliness, through the knowledge of Him who called us by glory and virtue, by which have been given *to us exceedingly great and precious promises, that through these you may be <u>partakers of the divine nature</u>.* (2 Peter 1:3-4)

God is Spirit. You and I carry God's very life. This is why Paul could say…. *"For me to live <u>is Christ."</u>*

It's important that we understand why the New Testament writers separated soul and spirit. Soul has to do with our behavior, our mental, emotional, and reasoning activities. Our spirit has been changed, and with that change came a new identity. When we placed our trust in Jesus Christ, as God in the flesh, who gave his life for our sins and was resurrected by the Father to new life which we now share—at that instant we became someone we had never been before. It is only through an understanding of our spiritual nature that the word of God through the scripture gives us the totality and the finality of what he has done for his children.

The scripture is filled with examples of the life-changing results of what God intended and designed to go along with the believer's moment of salvation.

1. We are **a new creation**—unique and one-of-a-kind.

….if anyone is in Christ, he is <u>a new creation</u>; old things have passed away; behold, <u>all things have become new</u>. (2 Corinthians 5:17)

2. We are **complete**—our spirit-person is not only a new creation, but that new creation is complete. Whatever age we became a believer, God identified us in

Christ's death, burial, and resurrection. We now have his new, and resurrected life as our life.

....you are complete in Him, who is the head of all principality and power. (Colossians 2:10)

....our old man was crucified with Him, that the body of sin might be done away with, that we should no longer be slaves of sin. (Romans 6:6)

3. We are **righteous**—simply because our newly created spirit is joined to God's Spirit. Our spirit & God's Spirit are in union.

....For He made Him who knew no sin to be sin for us, that we might become the righteousness of God in Him. (2 Corinthians 5:21)

It is because of God that you are in Christ Jesus.... This means that he made us righteous and holy, and he delivered us. (1 Corinthians 1:30)

4. We are **saints**—saints in the purest of terms. Not future saints, but present saints. Yes, saints who still occasionally commit sins. But saints whose sins are forgiven—he remembers our sins no more.

To the saints in Ephesus, the faithful in Christ Jesus.... Grace to you and peace from God our Father. (Ephesians 1:2)

To the saints and faithful brethren in Christ who are in Colossae: Grace to you and peace from God our Father and the Lord Jesus Christ. (Colossians 1:2)

5. We are **joint heirs with Christ**—God is our Father, Jesus is the heir of all things and we are his bride.

The Spirit Himself bears witness with our spirit that we are children of God, and if children, then heirs—heirs of God and joint heirs with Christ. (Romans 8:16-17)

6. We are **the elect**—chosen in Christ before the Lord formed the world. He knew us in our mother's womb and we were set apart to become a part of his family.

Who shall bring any charge against God's elect when it is God Who justifies—that is, Who puts us in right relation to Himself? Who shall come forward and accuse or impeach those whom God has chosen? (Romans 8:33)

7. We are **holy and blameless**—we may not always feel blameless or behave to our expectations of holiness, but in our union with him we are holy and blameless.

Even as in His love He chose us—actually picked us out for Himself as His own—in Christ before the foundation of the world, that we should be holy—consecrated and set apart for Him—and blameless in His sight, even above reproach, before Him in love. (Ephesians 1:4)

8. We are **a royal priesthood**—we are royalty and by that we have full access to the Father—24/7. He takes pleasure in our coming to him for anything.

....you are a chosen race, a royal priesthood, a holy nation, a people who are God's own possession. You have become this people so that you may speak of the wonderful acts of the one who called you out of darkness into his amazing light. (1 Peter 2:9)

9. We are **perfected forever**—we are spiritually flawless. We are one with God's Spirit and made spiritually perfect forever, because our spirit is joined with his Spirit. We must fully grasp that it is finished! Done!

....he has <u>*perfected forever*</u> *them that are sanctified.* (Hebrews 10:14)

You say..... "Well, God is still working on me!" Of course he is. He is changing the way you think, feel, and choose as you learn the ways of Christ.

Repent means to rethink. We are called to trust and live in the truth, and to make choices that advance God's ways, purposes, and kingdom.

> # We are called to renew our mind—to "rethink" who we are.

Do not be conformed to this world any longer with its superficial values and customs, but be transformed and progressively changed as you mature spiritually, by <u>*the renewing of your mind,*</u> *focusing on godly values and ethical attitudes, so that you may prove for yourselves what the will of God is, that which is good and acceptable and perfect in His plan and purpose for you.* (Romans 12:2)

God is committed to bringing us in line with his will for us, as we learn to make the good choices that carry the benefits of peace and rest in a troubled world.

For God is working in you, giving you the desire and the power to do what pleases him. (Philippians 2:13)

In short—we're all learning to re-think and flesh out who we are as God's children. That is Christian growth and maturity.

The wonderful British author Ian Thomas said…."*Most Christians spend their life trying to become who they already are.*" Dare I say it—saints!!

10. Here is the clincher! **He is our Life!**

It is the indwelling Spirit of God that brings us eternal life—His Life. Being joined to God's Spirit is to be joined to eternal life. When we were born again we were given God's very life. God is Spirit and he has come to live in our spirit to give us his life.

> # Christ is not just our Savior and Lord.
> ## *He is our LIFE.*

We were reconciled to God through the death of His Son, much more, having been reconciled, we are saved by His life. (Romans 5:10)

He who has the Son has life; he who does not have the Son of God does not have life. (1 John 5:12)

I came that they might have life, and that they may have it abundantly. (John 10:10)

Finished Means Finished

To close this section, let's review who we are again. The purpose of knowing and accepting our God-given identity is so we can separate who we are from how we sometimes think, feel, and too often make poor choices.

We are:

- a new creation
- complete
- righteous
- a saint
- holy and blameless
- joint heirs with Christ
- the elect
- a royal priesthood
- perfected forever
- a receiver of God's life

That is our present and eternal spiritual condition. It cannot change. God has committed himself to us for all of eternity. That is a biblical fact and it should drive everything in our primary belief system, resulting in the basic motivation for how we live moment-by-moment, and day-by-day during our time on this planet.

God is building a mansion for each of us and we must not lose sight of the materials that we are sending up for him to construct our mansion.

He has given us the foundation on which we must now build. In his gracious mercy he has arranged, through the death of his only son Jesus Christ, a full and total payment for all of our sins—past, present, and future. We are forgiven, reconciled back to a fulfilling and healthy relationship with our creator God. There is nothing we can add to his gift of salvation. But we must accept his call to us to build on the foundation he has provided for each of us.

Anyone who builds on that foundation may use a variety of materials—gold, silver, precious stones, wood, hay, or straw. But on the judgment day, fire will reveal what kind of work each builder has done. The fire will show if a person's work has any value. (1 Corinthians 3:12-13)

He tells us clearly that our good works, our character, our integrity, our relationships, our parenting, and our commitment to his ways are all sending up materials for our eternal mansion. Gold, silver and precious stones will stand up against the fire of his judgment day. Wood, hay, and straw represent those things that are self-centered and selfishly motivated. They will quickly be burned away at the judgment. We must commit to sending up good constructive materials.

Sowing and Reaping

There is one more responsibility that we must accept and learn to live by, for our own personal benefit. God has set in motion a principle that cannot be avoided in our life here on earth. That principle is, we will reap what we sow.

Do not be deceived, God is not mocked; for whatever a man sows, this he will also reap. (Galatians 6:7)

The world refers to that principle as, "what goes around, comes around." In all simplicity God tells us that if we sow anger, we will reap anger. If we sow love, we will reap love. If we sow generosity, we will reap generosity.

Should we not see clearly that it is God's purpose, and our interest, to sow well and to generate good materials for our eternal mansion.

And never underestimate the devil, a clearly defined enemy to God's ways.

Be sober, be vigilant; because your adversary the devil walks about like a roaring lion, seeking whom he may devour. (1 Peter 5:8)

God has him on a leash, but he knows our weaknesses. He can influence our thinking by taking advantage of our fleshly thoughts and desires and he can be convincing in pressing us to rationalize our reasoning and justify intentions and actions that in our heart of hearts we know are not in line with what God asks of us.

We have many "highways" that run through our mind and the devil knows which ones lead to anxiety, anger, lust, greed and the works of the flesh.

The devil is clever when he plays with our mind. He is the one that feeds our self-talk with lines like, "you are truly a failure" or "no one really loves you" or "you can't do anything right."

We live in a culture that has just about everything and yet even our churches are filled with believers whose self worth is in the tank. And most of it based on how they think others see them.

Remember—if you're looking to others for your self-esteem, hang this on your mirror. *What others think of me is nothing more than an opinion.* Let that sink in every day. It is just someone's opinion.

≈ ≈ ≈ ≈ ≈ ≈ ≈

Acceptance means you are valuable just as you are. It allows you to be the real you. You are not forced into someone else's idea of who you are. It means your ideas are taken seriously since they reflect you. You can talk about how you feel inside, why you feel that way, and someone really cares. Acceptance means you can try out your ideas without being shot down.... You feel safe. No one will pronounce judgment on you even though they don't agree with you. It doesn't mean you'll never be corrected or shown to be wrong. It simply means it's safe to be you and no one will destroy you out of prejudice.

—— Gladys M. Hunt

Part II

The Trials of Life

*....whenever you face trials of any kind, consider it
nothing but joy, because you know that the testing
of your faith produces endurance; and let endurance
have its full effect, <u>so that you may be mature</u>
and complete, lacking in nothing. (James 1:2-4)*

*When trials come your way be glad.
There is joy ahead, even though you must endure for a
while. Your testing and trials will show that your faith
is genuine. It's like fire tests and purifies gold.
And <u>the maturing of your faith</u> is far more precious
than gold. So let your faith hold firm
and stay strong through every trial.
The day is coming when your faithfulness will bring you
much praise and honor on that great day when
Jesus Christ is revealed to the whole world.*
(1 Peter 1:6-7)

Part One was filled with the totality of what God has done for us—the rest of the Good News we might say.

That good news however would be incomplete if we didn't look closely at the tension between what we can do ourselves as we grow and mature in our faith and understanding of God, and the tests and trials that God allows into our lives that he uses to develop and build our trust and reliance on him.

We are all aware of verses like Paul's statement in his letter to the Roman church....

And we know [with great confidence] that God [who is deeply concerned about us] causes all things to work together [as a plan] for good for those who love God, to those who are called according to His plan and purpose. (Romans 8:28 AMP)

But when things don't go our way—we lose our job, both cars break down, the furnace goes out, or all three kids need braces and our insurance doesn't cover it— just how does God's eternal plan for me seem to work all of that for my good?

Well he does, and no one could know better than Paul, who suffered stonings, beatings with rods, whipped with twenty-nine lashes, snakebite, shipwreck, and endless criticism, attacks, and death threats. Paul found that even in what seems to be an unreasonable tragedy God is in the mix, working his will and purpose in our lives, by stretching our faith and trust in him, and learning to relinquish our dependence on ourselves.

We lost one of our daughters a few years ago and know the agony of grief and loss. We know what it means to want to know the why, the possible purpose, and the relentless calling of God to cold turkey trust him in all things.

> ## Troubles are often the tools by which God fashions us for better things.
> —Henry W. Beecher—

Here is a definition of faith who came from a friend who is a nationally known minister and has also suffered times of tragedy in his own family.

"Faith is believing <u>the unreasonable</u>, because someone else, in whom we have absolute confidence, said it was so, and upon his word, we believe it, without asking for any further proof."

Those are comforting words in times of tragedy and loss. At times when we grasp at anything that might give us insight to the question, "Why God?"

Let's look deeper into the day-in-day-out challenges and trials of life that come at us out of the blue, rock our very world, and cause us to question our God who often seems to do very unreasonable things that impact our lives at very inopportune times.

What About Us Needs Work?

Our enemy, the devil, is quick to accuse all of us of our seeming failure when we fall short of God's standards. As the wonderful British writer Ian Thomas said…. "God loves failures….." What we must learn to rely on is the reality that our true identity, our spiritual being, is complete, perfect, holy, and righteous because our spirit is one with God's Spirit. Of course that leaves our soul—how we think, feel, and make choices, and that is in need of some serious work. And God is at work with each of us individually to bring about our maturity, our Christian growth, so that we learn to flesh out our real identity.

Paul said in his letter to the church at Rome, …*don't be conformed to this world, but be transformed by the renewing of your mind.* (Romans 12:2)

Part of that learning process is to accept who we are as God's called people. That begins by learning to think differently about who we are and the ultimate purpose for each of us as we journey through this world.

God uses the circumstances of life from the outside and the Holy Spirit within us to mould and shape us to trust and rely on his ways as we are faced with positive and negative events that cross our path.

What is God really up to in this dilemma I am facing right now?

Only God Knows Where to Tinker

There are many versions of a story about a brilliant German-born electrical engineer by the name of Charlie Steinmetz and his encounter with Henry Ford. I don't know which of the stories is accurate, but in each case the principle is the same, so I will relate the version I recall.

In the early days of the Ford Motor Company's development of a production line to mass produce automobiles, the requirements for the electrical engineering were very demanding. On one given day the entire production facility shut down and went dark. Of course idle workers brought a degree of panic and anxiety to Henry. After numerous attempts by his people to bring the plant back to full operation, Ford was reduced to calling for Charlie, who some say worked with General Electric at the time.

Charlie came over to the plant and after mastering what was needed to bring power back into the operation, the plant was once again alive with its line of new automobiles flowing through the production line.

Within a few days, Henry received a bill for Charlie's work in the amount of $10,000.00. Henry was surprised at the amount and wrote across the bill, "Isn't this a lot for just some tinkering around?" And he sent it back to Charlie. A few more days went by and Henry received a second bill which read....

Tinkering around — $1.00
Knowing where to tinker
$9,999.00

Word has it that Henry paid the bill.

How does that fit with what I am trying to say about how God is always at work in your life to teach you his ways? Very simply, the indwelling Holy Spirit knows precisely where to tinker to bring your mind, emotions, and will into line with your identity—who you are as his child.

The prime question to us is always—are we willing to trust him and cooperate with him as we learn his ways?

As Paul revealed in his letter to the church at Rome —there are times when we all still do things we don't want to do and times when we don't do things we know we should do. But as he concluded, those actions do not change who we are. Paul was faithful and clear to always separate our personhood from our behavior and actions.

The Flesh Stinketh

God made it clear in his Word that we have three enemies....always pushing us away from God's ways.

The world - the flesh - the devil. No matter how much we try to avoid those three enemies, each of them pulls us away from the ways of the Lord, influenced 24/7 by the power of sin that is always at work in our thinking and choices.

Of those three enemies I would suggest the most influential work that is done to us is through the subtle influences of what the scripture refers to as "the flesh."

For the flesh sets its desire against the Spirit, and the Spirit against the flesh; for these are in opposition to one another, so that you may not do the things that you please. (Galatians 5:17)

In The Message the same extended passage reads as a good explanation of what we all deal with on a daily basis.

My counsel is this: Live freely, animated and motivated by God's Spirit. Then you won't feed the compulsions of selfishness. For there is a root of sinful self-interest in us that is at odds with a free spirit, just as the free spirit is incompatible with selfishness. These two ways of life are antithetical, so that you cannot live at times one way and at times another way according to how you feel on any given day. It is obvious what kind of life develops out of trying to get your own way all the time. (Galatians 5:17-24)

So, we see that our spirit and soul are involved in a constant warfare with the world, the flesh, and the devil. The way we think, feel, and make choices all have tendencies and are somewhat spring-loaded to yield to the pull of the three enemies that work with the power of sin to keep us from yielding to the ways of the Lord.

Again, the following passage from The Message brings us face-to-face with the reality of how we are to deal with this battle within.

You must not give sin a vote in the way you conduct your lives. Throw yourselves wholeheartedly and full-time—remember, you've been raised from the dead!—into God's way of doing things. Sin can't tell you how to live. After all, you're not living under that old tyranny any longer. You're living in the freedom of God. So, since we're free in the freedom of God, can we do anything that comes to mind? Hardly. there are some acts of so-called freedom that destroy freedom. Offer yourselves to sin, for instance, and it's your last free act. But offer yourselves to the ways of God and the freedom never quits. All your lives you've let sin tell you what to do. But thank God you've started listening to a new master, one whose commands set you free to live openly in his freedom!

You can readily recall, can't you, how at one time the more you did just what you felt like doing—not caring about others, not caring about God—the worse your life became and the less freedom you had? And how much different is it now as you live in God's freedom, your lives healed? (Romans 6:12-19 Selected portions)

Many of the trials that we face as Christians are simply God's way of exposing our self-centered ways. God knows every thought we have.... every motive of our heart.

— 38 —

Sowing and Reaping

We must never lose sight of one of the great infallible principles that God has put in place throughout our entire universe. Let me again remind you....

Don't be misled—you can't mock the justice of God. You will always reap what you sow. (Galatians 6:7)

Sow love — reap love

Sow anger — reap anger

Sow judgment — reap judgment

Sow compassion — reap compassion

The LORD's light penetrates the human soul, exposing every hidden motive. (Proverbs 20:27)

I, the LORD, search all hearts and examine secret motives. (Jeremiah 17:10)

God alone examines the motives of our hearts. (1 Thessalonians 2:4)

God knows the secrets of every heart. (Psalm 44:21)

For he will bring our darkest secrets to light and will reveal our private motives. (1 Corinthians 4:5)

God's focus is to teach us to be willing to live our lives His way. In that endeavor God is as interested in doing something "in" us as doing something "through" us.

Our personal interior designer is re-decorating us from the inside/out. Like any good designer he will tear down in order to rebuild us to conform to his ways. He will pull down some walls and others will see in as he goes about his business. The process opens the eyes of our understanding to see what we are apart from what He is, and wants to be in us. He will break us of our self-ish ways which are at war with his Spirit within.

The Scripture is filled with God's methods of self-discovery—what we look like when we let "self" have its way. Coming up short is something we all experi-ence as children, as spouses, as parents, as friends.

Failure of Self Has Good Company

If you think coming up short is being a failure that God can't love, well you're in pretty good company. The following list has been around for some time, some lists more inclusive than others, but this conveys the point.

Jacob was a cheater,

David had an affair,

Noah got drunk,

Isaiah was a man of unclean lips

Jonah ran from God,

Paul was a murderer,

Gideon was insecure,

Martha was a worrier,

Thomas was a doubter,

Sara was impatient,

Elijah was moody & depressed

Moses stuttered,

Zacchaeus was short,

Abraham was old,

and Lazarus was dead.

.....God loves Failures

We all have weaknesses. Satan knows them all. But God uses those weaknesses to expose our self-centered motives, our selfish ways.

> ## What really matters is what happens *in* us, not *to* us.
> ## —James W. Kennedy—

His strength is made perfect..... in our weakness.

My power is being perfected and is completed and shows itself most effectively in your weakness. (2 Corinthians 12:9)

Here's the hard part to what God is up to. He will offend our mind, our reasoning, to develop and expand our faith.

In a nutshell here is Basic Christianity 101, as stated by a friend:

Truth - is what God says

Faith - is acting like God tells the truth

I've read the Bible thru many times. I'm always surprised at the things God does to help his children see what we are apart from his person and his ways.

Let me take you on a little tour of how God works with those he loves. I just want to jog your memory of some of God's choice people as God exposed their self-centered control issues as he brought them into a greater dependence upon himself and his ways.

Isaiah

Isaiah was told to take off all his clothes and go naked for three years. Hmmmm. Probably wasn't at the top of Isaiah's list of things to draw him closer to God. It just seems reasonable to wonder, Why?

Then God said, "Just as my servant Isaiah has walked around town naked and barefooted for three years <u>as a warning sign to Egypt and Ethiopia</u>, so the king of Assyria is going to come and take the Egyptians as captives and the Ethiopians as exiles. He'll take young and old alike and march them out of there naked and barefooted, exposed to mockery and jeers—the bared buttocks of Egypt on parade!" (Isaiah 20:3-4)

Don't you suppose there were times when Isaiah, from behind a tree somewhere, said, "Lord, what exactly is the plan here? Where are we going with this?"

Hosea

God, the sovereign judge of immorality, tells the prophet Hosea to go and marry a prostitute by the name of Gomer.

Go and marry a prostitute, so that some of her children will be conceived in prostitution. This will illustrate how Israel has acted like a prostitute by turning against the Lord and worshiping other gods. (Hosea 1:2)

You have to admit, that's a zinger. Really Lord? How about I just gather some folks in each little village and tell them your idea and we'll trust that the word will spread?

Jacob

Jacob worked for his Uncle Laban for seven years to gain the hand of his love Rachael, who was one of Laban's daughters. There was a wedding, a feast, and I would imagine that Laban made sure everything went according to plan. After dark he likely escorted his daughter to the honeymoon tent.

Then we read this passage....*And it came to pass, in the morning, behold, it was Leah....* (Genesis 29:25)

Leah was Rachael's sister! Bummer! Of course, Jacob was angered by the deception of his uncle, but he was so smitten by Rachael that he agreed to work another seven years for his unprincipled uncle.

As you read through this account, you have all sorts of thoughts. Strange that Jacob didn't notice until morning. I suppose this became a reference case for those who first had the idea of dating.

But God had much to do to break Jacob's selfish tendencies. Even in his mother's womb the scriptures tell us that he struggled with his brother.

Jacob's very name meant "cheater." He was deceitful and calculating. After he worked another 7 years for his nasty uncle he won the hand of his Rachel. Yet we learn that she died young. A setup for bitterness over the seven years that he might have had with the love of his life.

Jacob continued to wrestle with God however and was crippled for life because of it.

Jacob wrestled with a man until daybreak. When the man saw that he couldn't get the best of Jacob as they wrestled, he deliberately threw Jacob's hip out of joint. Jacob said, "I'm not letting you go 'til you bless me." The man said, "What's your name?" And he said, "Jacob." The man said, "Your name is no longer Jacob. From now on it's Israel. You've wrestled with God and you've come through." The sun came up as he left, limping because of his hip which was thrown out of joint. (Genesis 32:24-32 Selected)

Jacob's story can offend our reasoning. Yet in the end Jacob was a broken and softened man, as he became compassionate, trusting, transparent by learning to deny his selfish desires and do things God's way.

God's Plan for His Chosen

God has a plan to change those who are his from the inside/out.

Fix your attention on God. You'll be changed from the inside out. ....God brings the best out of you and develops maturity in you. (Romans 12:2)

Consider Noah, Jonah, Job and the Prophets of old. If you're looking for a reasonable and manageable God, you'll be disappointed. He will offend your mind and challenge all of your reasoning powers.

....my thoughts are not your thoughts, your ways are not my ways, says the LORD. (Isaiah 55:8)

In other words, God reminds us that he does things that are often contrary to the way we would do them. If the word "offend" offends you, keep reading. It is a word the Lord himself used.

Moses

Moses grew up with power. The resources of all of Egypt were to become available to him. But ultimately he drew on that fleshly power as his source. He took revenge, killed an Egyptian, was caught in the act and went from the palaces of Pharoah to the back side of the desert for forty years.

God had to expose that self-reliant streak in order to bring Moses into a reliance and dependence on him.

D.L. Moody once said....

> **"Moses spent forty years thinking he was somebody, forty years finding out he was nobody, and forty years finding out what God can do with a nobody."**

A natural leader, yet God had a plan and put Moses in the desert for 40 years with a million-plus grumbling Israelites. A plan Moses, and you and I, would never have conceived. But the exact plan that God, in his infinite wisdom, knew it would take to break through the controls and stubbornness and lead to the man God could use for his people.

Joseph

If God had said to Joseph, "How would you like to be Pharoah's vice president, in charge, top of the nation's ladder? Joseph likely would have said, "I like your idea God!" Except God went on, "Good, good, Joseph, now here's the plan, son. I'm going to have your brothers sell you to some bad dudes—slave traders to be exact. You'll end up spending twelve or thirteen years in jail. Your Dad will think your dead because I still have some work to do in him."

Don't you suppose Joseph would have ventured a question, like "Uh, excuse me God, but could we take a look at a Plan B, maybe?" But God was seeking brokenness in Joseph which in numerous dictionaries includes definitions like *subdued, weakened, humbled.*

Well, let's jump to the New Testament to see if God changed his tactics with his more contemporary followers.

James

Consider the example of James and his family. His brother was the Apostle John. His mother had asked Jesus if her two sons could join him and have a place of honor in his kingdom. Jesus said yes, but "you don't know what you are asking. Are you able to drink the cup that I am about to drink?" They joined his ministry.

Sometime later, James gets his head cut off for following Jesus. He was the first of the apostles to be martyred.

Later still, Peter ends up in prison. They all lived in close communities, so word was out that Herod, realizing that he had general approval when he killed James, figured, Peter will add even more to my popularity. But God sends an angel and Peter is miraculously freed from prison, saved from death.

Now, what do you think James' mother was thinking when she heard the news about Peter being free? Don't you suppose her first thought was, "Really, Lord. Wasn't my son as precious as Peter? Wasn't my James worth saving?"

Can you get a glimpse of why God says, *....the just shall live by faith? ....my ways are not your ways.*

The more unreasonable it is in our rational thinking processes, the more we have to trust Him in our true belief systems that we hold in our heart of hearts.

Why did 11 of the 12 apostles die horrible deaths God? I believe God's response is always, "Trust me. Cold turkey, trust me!"

But without faith it is impossible to walk with God and please Him, for whoever comes near to God must believe that God exists and that He rewards those who diligently seek Him. (Hebrews 11:6)

John the Baptist

Roaming, preaching, and baptizing those who would place their faith in the coming savior, John built up a well known, and pretty well received ministry with a large following.

Suddenly in the midst of his preaching John realizes that the one he is calling for people to place their faith in is actually here. He alone is the one who takes away the sins of the world—the Christ.

John graciously turns his ministry over to Jesus, loses his personal following, and is now down to just a few friends. Ultimately John ends up in jail, put there by Herod.

Now remember, Jesus is John's cousin and as far as we know Jesus never visited him in jail, and John's faith in Jesus as the savior, began to waiver.

So John sends some of his remaining followers to go to Jesus as ask, "Is he really the Christ?"

Jesus answered and said to them, "Go and tell John the things you have seen and heard: that the blind see, the lame walk, the lepers are cleansed, the deaf hear, the dead are raised, the poor have the gospel preached to them. And blessed is he who is not offended because of Me." (Luke 7:22-23)

> # Our faith, trust and heart must take us places where our mind can't go.

I believe Jesus was saying, "....don't be offended John, your mind can't fully grasp or understand the purposes of God. But trust me, I have everything under control."

Of course, Herod, who had heard of Jesus' miracles and feared his power, thought John might, in fact, be Jesus.

In the end, Herod's wife, who had been previously married to Herod's brother, convinced their daughter Salome to ask for John's head in response to Herod's desire to give her anything she requested as a thank you for her dancing. And John was beheaded to please Herod's wife and daughter.

Nothing rational about any of it. But it does require that we learn to trust with our heart—our deepest belief systems.

...if you confess with your mouth the Lord Jesus, and <u>believe in your heart</u> that God has raised him from the dead, you will be saved. (Romans 10:9)

Paul

How would God prepare Paul's heart.... to trust Him fully? To stand firm in his faith during the coming stonings, shipwreck, ridicule, jail, and persecution?

Paul was pretty crusty. A well trained, type A personality, and a strong leader. After his conversion he returned to Jerusalem at least twice wanting to work with the disciples. Both times they sent him back to the field, so to speak. God had to expose, prune, mold, break, shape, and humble this powerful man before he was ready to go out and speak with the heart and mind of God.

Paul is such a great example of God's patience as he works through circumstances and his indwelling Spirit to bring us in line with his ways.

This incredible process was reflected in Paul's own writings.

• 56 A.D. - When Paul visited the original apostles in Jerusalem, he stated in his letter to the Galatians, *....the leaders of the church had nothing to add to what I was preaching. By the way, their reputation as great leaders made no difference to me...* (Galatians 2:6)

• 5 years later in his first letter to the Corinthians, *....I am the least of all the apostles, and not worthy to be called an apostle....* (1 Corinthians 15:9)

• Later that same year his view of himself was further adjusted in his letter to the Ephesians, *....I am the least deserving Christian there is....* (Ephesians 3:8)

• Another five years later, writing to Timothy, *....Jesus came into the world to save sinners, and I am the worst of them all.* (1 Timothy 1:15) i.e. *I hold the record.*

A classic saint, who began to see his self-centered ways. The greatest of the Apostles had to come to the reality that, *....apart from Christ, I am nothing.* (John 15:5)

Peter

One minute Peter was ready to take on the Roman army, and an hour later, he denied even knowing Christ.

Jesus had told Peter, *"I tell you the truth, Peter—this very night, before the rooster crows, you will deny three times that you even know me."* (Matthew 26:34)

All the world is a stage, wrote Shakespeare. And perched upon the fence for Peter was Mr. Rooster, primed and ready, created "for such a time as this."

Peter's third denial of his Lord came that night, and stage right, cue the Rooster. Stage left, the Lord comes out the door and catches Peter's eyes.

Oh my.... can you sense what Peter felt? Pain..... Anger..... Frustration...... Exposure! God had broken through and Peter began to see Peter—apart from his relationship with Christ.

The flesh. The pride. The lies. The motives. The failure. The maverick. Broken....

And Peter went out and wept bitterly... (Luke 22:62)

Truth often.... brings sorrow!

For godly sorrow that is in accord with the will of God produces change; but worldly sorrow, the hopeless sorrow of unbelievers, produces death. (2 Corinthians 7:10)

We are all somewhere in the process. God may be offending your mind, your reasoning. It always comes back to *trust and obey*. Trust opens the door to understanding.

By faith, an inherent trust and confidence in the power, wisdom and goodness of God, we understand....(Hebrews 11:3)

The flesh is a powerful force and one that we are never fully free from. We learn at an early age to control, manipulate, shade the truth, and get our way.

> # You don't know what
> # faith you have until it is tested.
> ## —Rees Howells—

When many Christians see references to "the flesh" in the Scriptures they automatically think of the body, skin, physical things. But in reality the flesh includes not only our body and all of its physical desires but also how we think, feel, and make choices. That is why we are told the flesh is at war with the Spirit.

Paul said to the Colossians.... *put to death and deprive of power the evil longings of your flesh with its sensual, self-centered instincts, immorality, impurity, sinful passion, evil desire, and greed, which is a kind of idolatry because it replaces your devotion to God. But now rid yourselves completely of all these fleshly things: anger, rage, malice, slander, and obscene, abusive, filthy, and vulgar language from your mouth.* (Colossians 3:5 & 8)

As believers we're always going upstream against

the systems of the world. Our culture just naturally opposes the ways of God, sometimes in subtle ways and sometimes blatantly.

For all that is in the world—the lust of the flesh, the lust of the eyes, and the pride of life—is not of the Father but is of the world. (1 John 2:16)

> **No man, for any considerable period, can wear one face to himself and another to the multitude without finally getting bewildered as to which may be the true.**
> —Nathaniel Hawthorne—

God seems to let us have our own way much of the time. When we finally hit a wall, or get into a box with no exit, then He is faithfully there to show us his way.

The scriptures show us that flesh always comes before Spirit. In the Old Testament....

Cain came before Abel

Ishmael came before Isaac

Esau came before Jacob

Saul came before David

In both Old and New Testaments it was often noted by a change in name, but the principle still applied....

Saul came before Paul

Simon came before Peter

Nearly forty years ago, I was having lunch in Florida with a man who had been introduced to me by a dear pastor friend. I had come to respect this conference leader whose insight and opinion I trusted and knew I could confidently rely upon.

During our conversation over lunch I asked my friend a very simple question. "You know me well enough to be honest with me," I said. "So tell me what you see in me that you believe the Lord wants to change or transform for his purpose."

My friend didn't hesitate before he explained to me that I had a tendency toward self-promotion. That I had an inclination to present what I now call "the imposter"—finding ways to present to others, a "pretender." He explained that he knew me well enough that I didn't need to do that and I must learn to rest in, and present, my true self to others, at all times. He graciously, and in his gentle way, assured me that underneath the imposter I was a kind and gracious person and only through that person would I gain the trust of others and be able to communicate in ways that would be used by the Lord.

God's timing is always perfect. I knew exactly what my friend was talking about and made a commitment that day that I would learn to rest in, and accept, who I was.

Was it difficult. Of course it was, and I still have tendencies to embellish when someone asks me a question about me.

My teen and early years were largely spent on a stage, where I learned to perform and create the person I wanted others to see. Whether acting, doing comedy, performing as a musician—I had learned well how to present the imposter.

But God has been faithful. Through the valleys of life we gradually come to see, like the apostle Paul, *I am the vine; you are the branches. The one who remains in me— and I in him—bears much fruit, because apart from me you can accomplish nothing.* (John 15:5)

The most powerful thing any Christian can do is fall before the Lord and give him the right to your life— hook, line, and sinker as they say. Total! 100%! Lord, I am yours and in the best way I know how, I want you to take charge of my life and teach me your ways that I might walk in them.

I am reminded of when Joshua took the Israelites across the Jordan. After the crossing Joshua was near the town of Jericho. He looked up and saw a man standing in front of him with sword in hand. Some believe it was Christ, others believe it was an angel. *Joshua went up to him asking "Are you friend or foe?" The man said.... "Neither one, I'm the commander of the Lord's heavenly forces." Joshua fell to the ground in reverence.* (Joshua 5:13-14)

My paraphrase of that is that Joshua realized he was in the presence of power and said, "Whose side are you on?" A natural response when face to face with God's authority. The man replied (my version)....

> ## "I'm not here to take sides.....
> ## I'm here to take over!"

And Joshua fell before him in total submission.

We all find it easy to say that God has a plan for our life. But trusting him with that plan is easily said, but seldom done in the midst of the stressors of life.

God is Getting Us Ready

As a friend of mine once noted....

God is fixin' to fix you.

But if you try to fix the fix

He's fixin' to fix you with,

He'll find another fix to fix you,

until you let the fix

He's fixed for you

...fix you!

On a more realistic note, the following was given to my wife and me many years ago to help us understand the ways of our Lord. It was written in long hand by our friend and counselor.

≈ ≈ ≈ ≈ ≈ ≈ ≈

"The trials of life are God's loving gift so that we can learn how great He is and how profoundly He has made His grace available to us. Our trials should not be looked on as a curse, but as a great blessing. He has allowed us to have these trials so we will learn of Him in ways that have not been made available to others."

— Dr. Victor Matthews

Part III

Maturity is the Goal

I don't count myself an expert in all of this,
but I leave the past behind and with hands outstretched
to whatever lies ahead I go straight for the goal.
(Philippians 3:14)

A portion of Part III is used with permission from the teaching of DeVern Fromke who passed along some of the insights I feel belong in this book. All of the men I noted in my Introduction have written excellent books and I would be remiss to not suggest that you go on line and purchase any of their works. Each of them crossed denominational lines and ministered to the body of Christ at large and will be rewarded for their work.

Mr. Fromke would likely have titled this section, *The Ultimate Intention,* which is the title of one of his books.

When we look at the New Testament as a whole, we must ask ourselves.... What is the primary message that God wants to convey to me?

A Targeted Purpose

When Paul said he was going *"straight for the goal"* what did he mean? Or what was the writer of Hebrews referring to when he wrote that *"solid food is for the mature, for those who have been trained by experience and practice to distinguish what is good for them."*

What was Jesus passing along to his disciples when he told them what was coming and what it would demand of him? *"The time has come for the Son of Man to be glorified. I tell you truly that unless a grain of wheat falls into the earth and dies, it remains a single grain of wheat; but if it dies, it brings a good harvest.* (John 12:24)

The scriptures teach that out of Christ's death came resurrection life. For his followers there is a measured cost to our maturity and, like Paul, we must set our eyes on the prize, the purpose of the road we are on. We must not get so bogged down with the trials of life that we lose sight of the larger purpose—God's ultimate goal.

Jesus said, *"The kingdom of God is like a man scattering seed on the ground and then going to bed each night and getting up every morning, while the seed sprouts and grows up, though he has no idea how it hap-*

pens. The earth produces a crop without any help from anyone: first a blade, then the ear of corn, then the full-grown grain in the ear. And as soon as the crop is ready, he sends his reapers in without delay, for the harvest-time has come." (Mark 4:28-29)

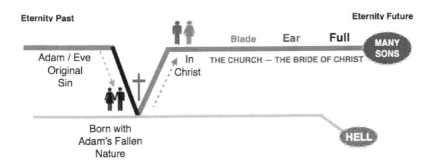

The *blade* represents the early church in many ways. Learning, questioning, and largely immature—needing the milk of the word. A new believer falls into the same pattern of need.

The *ear* represents the many facets of Christian growth to include wrestling with our natural independence and God's call for a weakened self and a stronger dependence on the indwelling Spirit and the promised access to the mind of Christ.

The *full-grown grain*, or full corn, represents our maturity in the faith. Our ability to trust in, rely on, and rest in the reality of God's grace and love for us without the guilt, stress and shame that God still needs "pay back" for all that he has done for us and in us.

The growth process can be difficult for us as humans on a fallen planet as we mature just as Jesus referred to in his example.

I spent my first twelve years on a farm in Iowa where corn was the primary crop that my father planted on our one-hundred-and-sixty acres. There was the constant need for rain, the fear of hail storms, fierce winds, and the long periods of just waiting for maturity, growth, and cooperating weather for the harvest.

To see the personal application of what Jesus was teaching, we must be prepared to be called upon, through the indwelling Holy Spirit, to experience what we claim to believe, by faith.

The Early and the Latter Rain

Let's look further into the graphic example with another insight that Mr. Fromke taught.

In the Middle Eastern and Oriental growing season there is the early rain, a rain in the spring to soften the soil for planting. And there is a latter rain, a rain in the fall to bring the harvest to fruition.

Be patient, brethren, until the coming of the Lord. See how the farmer waits for the precious fruit of the earth, waiting patiently for it until it receives the early and the latter rain. (James 5:7)

If we could apply the *early rain* as a pouring out of God's Spirit when he released the Holy Spirit to the church at Pentecost, then it is reasonable to believe that there will come a *latter rain* when God pours out his Holy Spirit for a great harvest before his return.

This is what the prophet Joel announced would happen: *"In the Last Days," God says, "I will pour out my Spirit on every kind of people: Your sons will prophesy, also your daughters; Your young men will see visions, your old men dream dreams. When the time comes, I'll pour out my Spirit on those who serve me, both men and women....* (Acts 2:17-18)

Learning Our Father's Ways

Bar, as in Bar Mitzvah, is a Jewish word literally meaning "son" and mitzvah means "commandment." Thus bar mitzvah literally translates to "son of commandment." In the Hebrew tradition, at five years old a son is required to study the Scriptures. At ten years he studies for the Mishnah, or the traditions of Jewish law. Then at 13 he is to focus on the commandments. The Talmud, the collection of Jewish doctrines and laws gives 13 as the age at which a boy's vows become legally binding. This then results in his becoming a "man" with its required responsibilities. The same is also true for daughters who mature to their full measure and their consequent Bat Mitzvah. Bat meaning daughter.

In a practical way there is a modern parallel in most homes in our western culture. As a child on an Iowa farm I spent most of my time with my dad. Whether with him on horse and wagon, tractor and plow, in the barn putting up hay and milking cows, or in the garden hoeing weeds and digging up potatoes —

I was in the process of learning my father's ways.

I learned to pump a tin cup full of water when I was thirsty, how to wipe mud and manure off my shoes, get over a barbed wire fence, lead a horse to the water tank, scoop shelled corn from the wagon to the corn bin, clean potatoes to go into the bin in the basement, eat a sun-warmed tomato right off the vine out in the garden, and how to defeather a chicken so my mother could get it ready for dinner. I learned my father's ways.

It's my understanding that there were ancient cultures, among them the Greeks and Romans, who would hire a tutor to come into the home to teach the son the father's ways to prepare him for manhood. This was often followed by an adoption ceremony where the father then officially adopted his own son. The process was complete and it was time for the child to become a son.

As Christians, no matter what age we receive Christ as our Savior and Lord, we also have a training period to learn the Father's ways. The indwelling Holy Spirit is our source and guide, our tutor if you will, as we move from being a child of God to becoming a son. Refer again to the illustration on a previous page—the blade, the ear, the full corn on the way to maturing and becoming full sons.

Most of this maturing process is mental. Learning the ways of God, developing our faith and trust and reliance on his strength and power in times of testing. Learning to think in terms of his thoughts and purposes.

For who has known the mind and purposes of the Lord, so as to instruct Him? But we have the mind of Christ, to be guided by His thoughts and purposes. (1 Corinthians 2:16)

...don't be conformed to this world any longer with its superficial values and customs, but be transformed and progressively changed as you mature spiritually by the renewing of your mind focusing on godly values and ethical attitudes....(Romans 12:2)

Praise be to God for giving us through Christ every possible spiritual benefit as citizens of Heaven! For consider what he has done—before the foundation of the world he chose us to become, in Christ, his holy and blameless children living within his constant care. He planned, in his purpose of love, that we should be adopted as his own children through Jesus Christ—that we might learn to praise that glorious generosity of his which has made us welcome in the everlasting love he bears towards the Son. (Ephesians 1:5-6)

And it is plain, too, that we who have a foretaste of the Spirit are in a state of painful tension, while we wait for *that redemption of our bodies and <u>the full realization of our sonship in him.</u>* (Romans 8:23)

All who follow the leading of God's Spirit <u>are God's own sons.</u> You're not meant to fall back into the old attitudes of fear and worry—<u>you have been adopted into the very family of God</u> and you can speak to him with a full heart—Father, my Father. (Romans 8:15)

Our Personal Interior Designer

Peter Lord suggested we consider the indwelling Holy Spirit as a personal interior designer. He is validation of God's commitment to mold and shape us into his own image as we learn his ways.

Between becoming a Christian and our full adoption there is growth, education, and discipline.

Mr. Fromke stated it well....

> **A child is one born of God.
> A son is one taught of God.
> A child has God's nature.
> A son has God's character.**

God's very life has been planted in us and we share his nature through our oneness with his Spirit. We are learning to deny the ways of the world and the ways of the flesh and to yield our life to his indwelling life as our source for everything.

It is much more than just being born into God's family. It is a preparation and attainment of responsibility in the kingdom of God. Our responsibility is to connect firmly in that process of moving from child to son.

We read this relevant verse from Isaiah every year at Christmas time....

For unto us a Child is born, Unto us a Son is given; And the government will be upon His shoulder. (Isaiah 9:6)

Isaiah was, of course, speaking of Jesus who in God's perfect time was born a child in Bethlehem, was trained and tested until, in his moment of recognized maturity, God moved him from child to son, as the heavens opened and John the Baptist heard the Father say....

"This is My beloved Son, in whom I am well pleased." (Matt 3:17)

Yes, even Jesus went through a learning and maturing process.

Isaiah said, in reference to the coming Immanuel— God with us....

Butter and honey shall he eat, that he may know to refuse the evil, and choose the good. (Isaiah 7:15)

Paul challenged the Roman believers.....

In my opinion whatever we may have to go through now is less than nothing compared with the magnificent future God has planned for us. The whole creation is on *tiptoe to see the wonderful sight <u>of the sons of God coming into their own</u>.* (Romans 8:18)

Paul also seemed to have this in mind in his letter to the Ephesians....

I pray that the eyes of your heart may be enlightened, so that you will know what is the hope of His calling, what are <u>the riches of</u> the glory of <u>His inheritance in the saints</u>, and what is the surpassing greatness of His power toward us who believe. (Ephesians 1:18-19)

Building Our Eternal Home

Here is what we must keep in the forefront of our thinking, God is committed to moving us into full sonship in ways that will bring honor and glory to him and the fulfillment of his kingdom purpose.

Our part is to learn his ways. His part is to mold and shape us from the inside out to reflect the fulness of his life within.

He was angry with Israel if you recall.....

Your fathers saw My works for forty years but I was angry with that generation. They always go astray in their heart, and <u>they did not know My ways</u>. (Hebrews 3:9-10)

There is a purpose in learning God's ways. Christ reminded us....

My father's house has many mansions and I go to prepare <u>a place for you</u>... (John 14:2)

I remind you again as Paul reminded us....

Each person needs to pay attention to the way they build on the foundation. Whether someone builds with <u>gold, silver, precious stones, hay, wood, and stubble</u>, each one's work will be clearly shown. Fire will test the quality of each one's work." (1 Corinthians 3:10-15)

When we do things God's way we're sending up the building materials that are going into our eternal home. The choices we make every day determine what those materials are.

We must learn to rely on God's commitment to our growth and maturity in ways that often go against what we desire for ourselves. Rather than resist his molding and shaping in our lives, we must learn to rejoice in it and be grateful that he loves us enough to accomplish his purpose even though he knows it is sometimes difficult for us to endure the discipline and correction we need.

Bear what you have to bear as "chastening"—as God's dealing with you as sons. No true son ever grows up uncorrected by his father. For if you had no experience of the correction which all sons have to bear you might well doubt the legitimacy of your sonship. After all, when we were children we had fathers who corrected us, and we respected them for it. Can we not much more readily submit to a heavenly Father's discipline, and learn how to live? (Hebrews 12:8-9)

The Master Pruner

Jesus reminded us of the value of God's hand in our shaping and maturing....

My Father is the vinedresser.... Every branch in Me that bears fruit, He prunes it so it may bear more fruit. (John 15:1)

What does that mean for you and for me on a day-to-day basis. Let me just give you a glimpse.

Nearly 40 years ago there was an ad in *National Geographic Magazine* for Gallo Wines. I first became aware of it from my friend Peter Lord.

I have kept a copy of the ad and used it often in my teaching. It is a concise and beautiful commentary on Jesus' teaching as recorded in John 15. I will give you a taste (pun intended) of what it takes to make good wine.

Quoting from the ad with my comments in parenthesis.... *Pruning—the cutting off of living parts of the grape vine—is one of the most important practices in the culture of grapes.* (Note that living parts must sometimes be removed)

...last year's wood must be pruned away. If too much wood is left on the vine, it will produce too many grapes to properly ripen. These grapes will tend to be green and harsh, both undesirable characteristics.... (Hay, wood, and stubble are not good end products for building)

No two vines are identical. Each one must be pruned differently. How old is the vine? Is it in vigorous health and should its crop be retained this year or sacrificed for the future good of the vine? Precisely where on the vine should spurs be permitted to grow? A master pruner must know all such things and care for each vine according to its own individual needs. (God is our Master Pruner and Vinedresser)

Thinning is the removal of enough grape clusters from the vine—eliminating part of the crop—to insure the quality of the remainder. Sometimes this can mean removing as much as one-half of the crop from an overproducing vine. (Good fruit is removed to assure better fruit)

That is why in the vineyards we do not consider a man thoroughly qualified until he has been pruning for at least three years under close supervision. Then we allow him to prune on his own, but always following the advice of a master pruner. (The disciples were with Christ for three years before their ministries flourished)

I trust you will see, and understand, the process you are in, and the ultimate purpose of your time on this earth as God's child and developing son. As you mature in your Christian growth you are learning to flesh out the mature person that God is preparing for ultimate sonship in his kingdom.

You are pleasing to God because of who you are—his chosen, adopted child. Nothing you can do will improve or enlarge his love for you. But what you can do will have an impact on the ultimate rewards that await your arrival into the eternal picture being prepared for you.

Know this—that in a race all the runners run their very best to win the prize So run your race in such a way that you may seize the prize and make it yours! Press on toward the goal of the heavenly prize of the upward call of God in Christ Jesus. (1 Corinthians 9:24 and Philippians 3:14)

≈ ≈ ≈ ≈ ≈ ≈ ≈

God whispers to us in our pleasures, speaks in our conscience, but shouts in our pains: it is his megaphone to rouse a deaf world. — C.S. Lewis

Final Thoughts

Fleshing out who we are by identity is the process of learning to trust and obey.

I must learn to live in my new, natural personhood who is complete in Christ.

When I am faced with a decision, I know immediately if it is not right for me. My spirit is unsettled and that is the real me in union with God's Spirit within. Good advice on this is—when in doubt.... don't!

I must learn to listen as closely as possible to the Spirit within. I must learn to trust what I discern to be right. And I must move in accordance with what I know to be the truth as given to me through the Scriptures that are a part of the guidance available to me from God himself.

I must learn to express my trust in God by releasing myself to follow through with the actions that are necessary to validate and express my true identity to the world around me—the people that God has placed in my life and those who bounce in and out of my life during the course of my average day.

To <u>look</u> is one thing.

To <u>see</u> what you look at

is another.

To <u>understand</u> what you see

is a third.

To <u>learn</u> from what you understand is still

something else.

But to <u>act</u> on what you learn

is what really matters, isn't it?

—Harvard Business Review

I must also learn to maintain my focus on the larger picture—the eternal purposes of God for me. There is a role I am called to play in the advancement of God's kingdom here on this earth. And I must keep in mind that my role has eternal meaning.

The following interesting story was taken from *Leadership Magazine.*

A young man who works in an aquarium explained that the most popular fish is the shark. If you catch a small shark and confine it, it will stay a size proportionate to the aquarium. Sharks can be six inches long yet fully matured. But if you turn them loose in the ocean, they grow to their normal length of eight feet. That also happens to some Christians. I've seen some of the cutest little six-inch Christians who swim around in a little puddle. But if you put them into a larger arena—into the whole creation—only then can they become great.

We must be willing to use our gifts, our skills, our education, our talents, and our purpose to express our commitment to attaining the goal set before us.

In Jesus' name, we make the decisions necessary to press on toward Christian maturity.

$$\approx \ \approx \ \approx \ \approx \ \approx \ \approx \ \approx$$

I know the plans that I have for you, says the Lord,

thoughts of peace and not of evil,

to give you a future and a hope.

(Jeremiah 29:11)

He knows the way that I take;

When He has tested me,

I shall come forth as gold.

(Job 23:10)

Made in the USA
Middletown, DE
07 August 2017